Contents

Our lives are full of words. You probably say about 6,000 to 8,000 words each day. You hear and read thousands more. From posters to schoolbooks, text messages to song lyrics—words are everywhere. We use them to communicate, learn, and have fun.

What is a word?

A word is something made up of a letter or group of letters that has a meaning, or definition. It is impossible to count the exact number of words we have in the English language—well-known dictionaries such as Webster's list around half a million words. Every word has a history, a meaning, and a structure.

What is word structure?

Words are made of parts, and the parts make up the structure. Letters of the alphabet are the smallest parts of words and are usually the first element we use to start to construct and read written words. Many words are made of a word with parts added to the beginning or end, such as greener (green-er). The word without the addition (green) is called the root word. The structure of a word is called its morphology.

It is important to know about the parts of words—their morphology—because it helps us to understand and read words, to pronounce them, and to use and spell them correctly.

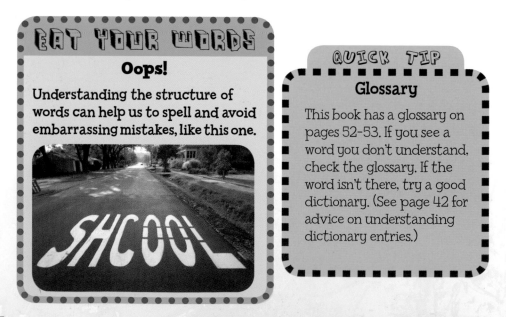

EAT YOUR WORDS

Oops!

Understanding the structure of words can help us to spell and avoid embarrassing mistakes, like this one.

QUICK TIP

Glossary

This book has a glossary on pages 52-53. If you see a word you don't understand, check the glossary. If the word isn't there, try a good dictionary. (See page 42 for advice on understanding dictionary entries.)

Find your way with words

The
Structure
of Words

Liz Miles

violet

im

ultra

mortal

bicycle

Heinemann LIBRARY

Chicago, Illinois

© 2013 Heinemann Library
an imprint of Capstone Global Library, LLC
Chicago, Illinois

To contact Capstone Global Library, please
call 800-747-4992, or visit our web site,
www.capstonepub.com

Edited by Andrew Farrow, Laura Hensley,
Vaarunika Dharmapala, Helen Cox Cannons
Designed by Philippa Jenkins
Original illustrations © Capstone Global Library
Ltd
Illustrated by Capstone Global Library Ltd
Picture research by Tracy Cummins
Production by Sophia Argyris
Printed in China by Leo Paper Products Ltd

17 16 15 14 13
10 9 8 7 6 5 4 3 2 1

**Library of Congress Cataloging-in-Publication
Data**
Miles, Liz.
  The Structure of Words : Understanding Prefixes,
Suffixes, and Root Words / Liz Miles.
      pages cm.—(Find your way with words)
  Includes bibliographical references and index.
  ISBN 978-1-4329-7656-9 (hb)—ISBN 978-1-4329-
7661-3 (pb) 1. English language—Suffixes and
prefixes. 2. English language—Word formation. I.
Title.

PE1175.M54 2014
425.92—dc23   2012039618

Acknowledgments
We would like to thank the following for
permission to reproduce photographs:
Alamy pp. 26 (© The Art Gallery Collection), 45 (©
Art Directors & TRIP); AP Photo p.4 (Kalamazoo
Gazette, Jill McLane Baker); Corbis p. 13 (©
Bettmann); Getty Images pp. 10 (Rosebud
Pictures), 11 (Samir Hussein), 22 (Franz Marc Frei);
Shutterstock pp. 5 (© Warren Goldswain), 7 (©
auremar), 8 (© Sheftsoff), 9 (© Alice Mary Herden
Green-Fly Media LLC), 14 (© wavebreakmedia),
17 (© James Steidl), 19 (© Binkski), 24 (©
Danomyte), 25 (© DEKANARYAS), 27 (© Roxana
Gonzalez), 28 (© Paul Hakimata Photography), 31
(© Shkvarko), 33 (© Luis Santos), 35 bottom left (©
Apaterson), 35 bottom right (© Howard Klaaste), 35
top left (© Grosu Valentyn), 35 top right (©
Iznogood), 37 (© violetkaipa), 39 (© MarchCattle),
40 (© Stiggy Photo), 41 (© Mopic), 43 (© Smit), 44
left (© Carlos E. Santa Maria), 44 right (© Vlue), 47
(© Arogant), 48 (© James Steidl).

Back cover photograph of a diamond reproduced
by Shutterstock (© James Steidl).

We would like to thank Joanna John for her
invaluable help in the preparation of this book.

Every effort has been made to contact copyright
holders of material reproduced in this book. Any
omissions will be rectified in subsequent printings
if notice is given to the publisher.

Disclaimer
All the Internet addresses (URLs) given in this
book were valid at the time of going to press.
However, due to the dynamic nature of the
Internet, some addresses may have changed, or
sites may have changed or ceased to exist since
publication. While the author and publisher regret
any inconvenience this may cause readers, no
responsibility for any such changes can be
accepted by either the author or the publisher.

Growing your vocabulary

When a child is about 18 months old, he or she probably uses around 50 words. Eight-year-olds understand about 6,000 root words. How many words do you think you can understand and spell? It will depend. The more you read, and the more you look up words in dictionaries, the bigger your vocabulary will become.

The letters of the alphabet are the building blocks we use to make words.

Putting words together

Learning how words are put together helps with reading, writing, and remembering spellings. There are many parts to words, each with their own name. This book looks at the parts listed below. You will know some of them already.

k

A consonant is any letter that involves some halting of airflow in pronunciation—except for y, which can be a vowel or consonant. In the word yak, it is a consonant.

t

There are 26 letters in the English alphabet. Each letter has a name and represents a sound. For example, the letter t makes the sound /t/, as here, in tickets. English has more sounds than letters in the alphabet, so some letters can make more than one sound.

Super

A prefix is a syllable or word at the front of a root word. It changes or adds to the meaning of the root word. Super has been added to the word show to explain that this show is extra-special.

f

A phoneme is a unit of sound when you speak. The word for has two phonemes in it: the /f/ sound and the /or/ sound (see page 8).

Buy your tickets for

Matt's Magical Supershow

EAT YOUR WORDS

Exceptions to the rules

Learning how words are put together helps us to spell. But there are exceptions to rules and common word structures, especially if the words are names. If in doubt, always look up a word in a dictionary or encyclopedia.

The designer of this T-shirt should have looked up how to spell the name Shakespeare, to avoid an expensive mistake. All the T-shirts printed with this mistake had to be taken out of the stores.

M

All letters exist as capital letters—also called uppercase letters (e.g., M), and lowercase letters (e.g., m). Here, a capital letter is used for a name and to start the sentence.

Mag

A syllable is a word, or part of a word, that has a separate sound when you say it (e.g., mag in magical). The word magical has three syllables in total (mag-i-cal).

Magical

A root word is the basic part of a word, from which others can be built. In magical, the root word is magic.

al

A suffix is a syllable or word at the end of a root word. It changes or adds to the meaning of the root word. For example, -al changes the noun magic into an adjective, magical.

o

The letters a, e, i, o, and u are vowels. Sometimes y acts as a vowel, such as in the word rhythm. All words in English contain at least one vowel.

sh

Graphemes are the letter or letters that represent the sounds (phonemes) in our language. For example, sh in supershow is one grapheme (see page 8).

7

It's How You Say It

Words are made up of one or more sound. The sounds are those you make with your lips and tongue as you speak or read aloud. They are also the sounds you say to yourself as you read silently.

Writing down sounds

In writing, one or more letters are used to represent the sounds (phonemes). The letters that represent each sound are called graphemes. Some graphemes might have:

2 letters   Example: ch in chat
3 letters   Example: igh in high
4 letters   Example: eigh in eight

When young children start to learn to read, they often split words into parts, or graphemes. Then they blend them together to read the whole word.

QUICK TIP

Check it!

Beware! Research has shown there are more than 1,700 ways of spelling the 44 phonemes! For example, the sound /oo/ has more spellings than those listed in the table below, such as: ough (through), ew (chew), ue (due). So when writing new words, always check their spelling in a dictionary.

Sounds and spellings

Some phonemes have different spellings. For example, the same /sh/ sound is spelled sh (as in ship), ch (as in chef), and ss (as in mission). By learning phonemes' most common spellings, you can figure out how to read lots of unfamiliar words. Whether you are aware of it or not, you probably know most of these spellings already.

Here are some examples of sounds (phonemes) and some of their most common spellings (graphemes). Read the examples and you will hear how the same sound is made using different graphemes:

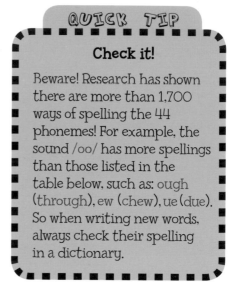

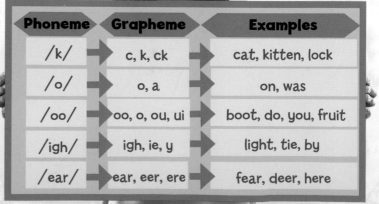

Phoneme	Grapheme	Examples
/k/	c, k, ck	cat, kitten, lock
/o/	o, a	on, was
/oo/	oo, o, ou, ui	boot, do, you, fruit
/igh/	igh, ie, y	light, tie, by
/ear/	ear, eer, ere	fear, deer, here

EAT YOUR WORDS

Phonemes

The small units of sound in spoken words are called phonemes. There are 44 phonemes in the English language.

QUICK TIP

Break and blend

Splitting words into graphemes is a good way to read words you don't know. For example, reading the word graphemes is tricky, so it is best to start by sounding out each part: g-r-a-ph-eme-s. Then blend the sounds to read the word. (Helpful hint: The letters eme make the sounds ee-m, as in seem.)

WORDS IN ACTION

Can you read the names of these dinosaurs? They are long, so split them into graphemes to help you! Under each name, there is a guide showing you how to split, say, and blend the graphemes.

Pachycephalosaurus
(P-a-ch-y-c-e-ph-a-l-o-s-aur-u-s)
pack-ee-seff-ah-low-sore-uss

Archaeornithomimus
(Ar-sch-ae-or-n-i-th-o-m-i-m-u-s)
ar-kee-or-nith-uh-my-mus

How do you say it?

Words or parts of words are pronounced differently in different English-speaking countries. For example, the following sentence can be read in different ways, depending on the native country of the speakers.

I didn't like *The Hungry Tomato* movie, either.

If the speakers are from the following countries, they would probably pronounce the letter a in tomato like this:

United States: /ai/ as in rain

United Kingdom: /ar/ as in cart

The i in fertile is often pronounced differently, too:

United States: /i/ as in ill

United Kingdom: /igh/ as in mile

Even if you don't live in New York, you are probably familiar with the accent from watching movies set there.

Tawk like a Noo Yawker

Sometimes actors or actresses exaggerate an accent to make the character they are playing more memorable or dramatic. For example, a New York character's words might be pronounced as shown in this table:

Standard English	first	mother brother	they, that, these	thirty-third	better
New Yorker	foist	mudda brudda	dey, dat, dese	toity-toid	bedduh

Regional accents

We all have an accent of some kind. People within different parts of a country often pronounce words differently. For example, in the eastern United States, many people pronounce the word aunt like "ah-nt." But in the Midwest, it is more commonly pronounced "ant."

Some parts of the country are known for particularly strong accents. For example, in Boston and some parts of New England, the /r/ sound is dropped in words like car and yard.

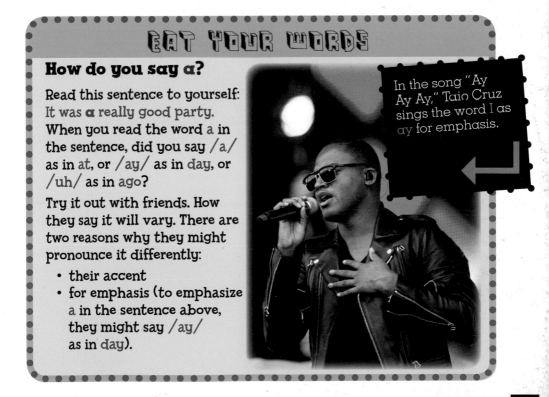

EAT YOUR WORDS

How do you say a?

Read this sentence to yourself: It was a really good party. When you read the word a in the sentence, did you say /a/ as in at, or /ay/ as in day, or /uh/ as in ago?

Try it out with friends. How they say it will vary. There are two reasons why they might pronounce it differently:

- their accent
- for emphasis (to emphasize a in the sentence above, they might say /ay/ as in day).

In the song "Ay Ay Ay," Taio Cruz sings the word I as ay for emphasis.

How do you pronounce that?

While it is important to know how to spell words, it is just as important to know how to say them! Many dictionaries give not only the meanings of words, but also their Standard English pronunciation.

Emphasis

Words can sound very odd if you emphasize the wrong part. Try putting the emphasis where the capital letters are in these words:

aweSOME   FANtastic

Now say the words normally. Because you know these words, you will put the emphasis where it should be:

AWEsome   fanTAStic

Some words have a different meaning depending on where you put the emphasis. The word record is an example:

- emphasis on the first part (RE-cord) makes it into a noun
- emphasis on the second part (re-CORD) makes it into a verb.

This tells you how to say the word. The capital letters (DAYL) show that you should emphasize this part of the word when you say it.

sesquipedalian (ses-kwuh-puh-DAYL-yuhn) *adjective* **1**. used to describe something as tall or big; "a sesquipedalian basketball player" **2**. used to describe very long words, with lots of syllables; "sesquipedalian scientific vocabulary" **3**. using long words, long-winded; "a sesquipedalian professor" *noun*: A long word.

These are the three possible meanings of the word if it is used as an adjective.

There is only one meaning of the word if it is used as a noun.

A dictionary will give you the meaning of a word. It will also show how a word is said.

Exceptions to the rules

A quick way to check the pronunciation of a word is to go online to the American Free Dictionary (www.thefreedictionary.com). Type in your word, click on Search, then click on one of the loudspeaker icons ◀ to hear pronunciations.

EAT YOUR WORDS

Advance or dance?

The clear pronunciation of all the parts of a word is important, or you might be misunderstood. During World War II (1939-1945), a spoken message was passed from soldier to soldier: Send reinforcements, we're going to advance. By the time the message got to the last soldier, it had become: Send three and four pence, we're going to a dance. (Pence are like British pennies.) So, unclear pronunciation can be disastrous!

We're going to a dance—send us money, please!

It's a mess

Standard English includes rules about how to sound out words according to their spelling. However, Standard English is not easy to learn, because there are so many unusual spellings. The same graphemes can have different sounds (such as ea in meat and great). The same sounds can have different graphemes or spellings (like the sound /z/ in zero and please).

Rule-breakers

Many of the words we read every day cannot be read by sounding out graphemes. Their graphemes do not represent sounds in the usual ways. We have to learn such words by sight. Examples are: the, said, who, their, and come.

Homophones

Lots of words sound the same, but have different graphemes. Here are a few:

there/their   here/hear   night/knight   see/sea   bare/bear

They are called homophones. Luckily, we can usually figure out what someone has said by using the context. If someone said goodnight to you on her way to bed, you would know she did not mean good knight (unless you had just killed a dragon!).

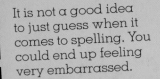

It is not a good idea to just guess when it comes to spelling. You could end up feeling very embarrassed.

Silent letters

Some letters in words are called silent letters because you cannot hear them. They hide at the beginning, end, and even in the middle of words!

k in knife, knee, knob
w in write, sword, answer
b in crumb, limb, doubt

Dialect

Characters in stories sometimes speak in dialect. The novel *To Kill A Mockingbird* is set in the 1930s in Alabama. The author, Harper Lee (born 1926), writes words as the characters speak, in southern dialects. Here is a quote in dialect from a character named Tom Robinson:

> I was just reachin' when the next thing I knows she—she'd grabbed me round the legs, grabbed me round th' legs, Mr. Finch. She scared me so bad I hopped down an' turned the chair over—that was the only thing, only furniture, 'sturbed in that room, Mr. Finch, when I left it.

From *To Kill a Mockingbird* by Harper Lee, published in 1960 by William Heinemann Limited. Reprinted by permission of The Random House Group Limited

Here are other words that appear in the book that are written as they are spoken:

wanta – want to	hafta – have to
yo' – you	yawl – you all
smatter – what's the matter?	'sturbed – disturbed

Dialect is useful in stories, but you should use Standard English for formal writing. Otherwise, few people will understand you.

Syllables and Vowels

Words are made up of one or more syllable. It is important to know about syllables, because they help us to spell and even to write poetry and song lyrics.

Every syllable has one vowel sound. The vowel sound can be made with:

- a single vowel: a, e, i, o, u, or y
- more than one vowel, such as: ee, ea, eau, a-e*.

(*a-e makes one syllable in words like date, where the a and e are separated by a consonant)

These words have one syllable:

cat, dog, wood, neat, steep

These words have two syllables. A line (/) is used to separate the syllables:

a/ffect, de/stroy, fa/ther, un/fold, back/ward

These are three-syllable words:

beau/ti/ful, char/act/er, pine/app/le

Words with more than one syllable are called multisyllabic.

WORDS IN ACTION

How many syllables?

To read long words correctly, it helps to split them into syllables. Split this long word into syllables to help you read it. How many syllables can you find?

Supercalifragilisticexpialidocious

Some people say it has 14 syllables, while others say 15. Those who say 15 pronounce the last letters, -cious, as two syllables (see-us) instead of one syllable (shus).

You should find it easier to read once you have split it up. This word is well known, but it does not have a definite meaning. It was written for the movie musical *Mary Poppins*. In the song, the character says it backwards—you could try that, too!

Diamond is a three-syllable word (di/a/mond). The a in the middle is unstressed and difficult to hear, since many people say di/mond.

Counting the syllables

Some vowel sounds are difficult to hear. To count the syllables in a word, say the word slowly, breaking it into parts. For example, in chocolate, the o in the middle is difficult to hear if you say the word fast. Vowels that are hard to hear are called unstressed vowels.

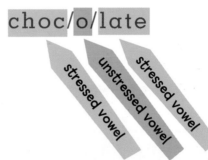

choc/o/late

stressed vowel
unstressed vowel
stressed vowel

There is an unstressed vowel in the following words, too. Each word has been split into vowels, and the unstressed vowel is in bold:

fuel (fu/**el**)
valuable (val/u/**a**/ble)
poem (po/**em**)
gardener (gard/**en**/er)

QUICK TIP

It helps to split words

Splitting words into syllables helps you to be a good speller. When you first read an unfamiliar word, split it into syllables and note all the vowels. You are then unlikely to miss some of the unstressed vowels when writing words. For example, people might misspell mystery as mystry because they forget the unstressed vowel (e) in the middle. But if they split it into syllables like this, they will remember the correct spelling: mys/ter/y.

Finding the rhythm

If you clap out the syllables in each word in a phrase, you will soon
discover that words have rhythm. Try it with these titles:

A/ven/gers A/ssem/ble
De/spi/ca/ble Me

The rhythm in phrases can have a big effect, so writers choose words
for the way they sound, in addition to their meaning. Look at the above
titles. Avengers and Assemble both have three syllables. Perhaps this
makes the title more memorable. The four-syllable Despicable makes
the weight of the rhythm fall on the one-syllable Me. Perhaps this helps
to make the little word Me sound more important and interesting.

Rhythm

Both rhythm and rhyme are important in poems. Some traditional forms
of poetry have a specific number of syllables in the lines. Some have
to be stressed and some have to be unstressed. Poets writing in a form
called iambic pentameter use this rhythm. Every second syllable is
stressed, and each line is usually made up of 10 syllables. To explain
it, it is often said to be like a heartbeat:

da-DUM, da-DUM, da-DUM, da-DUM, da-DUM.

The most famous playwright in the world, William Shakespeare, used
this form nearly 400 years ago for his plays. Spot the rhythm below,
especially in the second line. It gives the feel of an actor (player)
pacing around on a stage:

Life's **but** a **walking** shadow, a **poor player**
That **struts** and **frets** his **hour** upon the **stage**

Rap

Stressed syllables are used in song lyrics and in rap music to get the
musical beat. A rap rhythm is used in a poem called "The Boneyard
Rap" by Wes Magee. Here's the first verse:

This is the rhythmn
of the boncyard rap,
knuckle bones click
and hand bones clap.
Finger bones flick
and thigh bones slap,
when you're doing the rhythm
of the boneyard rap.
　　Woooooooo!

By permission of the author, Wes Magee

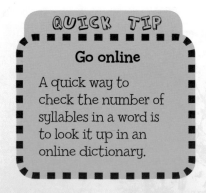

QUICK TIP

Go online

A quick way to
check the number of
syllables in a word is
to look it up in an
online dictionary.

Haiku

A haiku is a traditional Japanese form of poetry that paints a picture in the reader's mind in a few words. You can't write a haiku without counting syllables! It does not have to rhyme and is usually only three lines of five syllables, seven syllables, and five syllables each. People write haiku today to paint word pictures of the modern world:

> Freeway overpass...
> Blossoms in graffiti on
> fog-wrapped June mornings

By Michael R. Collings, from HAIKU for PEOPLE:
http://www.toyomasu.com/haiku/#world

In a dictionary entry like this, dots separate the syllables. This shows that tyrannosaurus has five syllables.

ty•ran•no•sau•rus te-raene'sorus/ *noun*
plural: ty·ran·no·sau·rus·es
a very large meat-eating dinosaur — called
also T. rex, tyrannosaurus rex /-rks/.

Rooting for Words

Many longer words have grown from smaller words. The smaller words are called root words. Root words hold most of the meaning of the longer words in which they appear. The root words in the longer words below have been highlighted:

shocking **comput**er **geo**graphy pre**made** bi**cycle**

Adding parts

The parts added to root words are called prefixes and suffixes:

- Prefixes are at the front of a root word (e.g., **super**sonic)
- Suffixes are at the end of a root word (e.g., shock**ing**).

One root word can appear in several different words, with prefixes or suffixes—or both.

Some root words stand alone as words. They have a meaning in themselves (for example, shock), but others are less likely to be used on their own (such as geo, which means "earth"). Spotting and understanding root words can help you spell longer words.

Compound words

Compound words are two or more separate words joined together. But there is still a root word in them. Words around the root word can be descriptive or change the meaning of the root word altogether.

Football

this tells you the type of ball

this is the root word

Can you spot the root word in these words?

Playground, farmyard, bedroom, blackberry, dragonfly

Find the answers on page 55.

biologist

a person who studies biology

biomass

the total amount (measured in mass) of living things in an environment

biome

a large community of plants and animals within a habitat

biology

the science or study of living things

bionic

something that is operated by electronics or machinery to make it lifelike

biography

a life story

Bio (meaning "life") is the root word in all of these longer words. When you come across new words that contain bio, you will know the word has something to do with life. You can then look at the context to figure out the meaning of the whole, longer word.

bio = life

QUICK TIP

Remember how to spell ...

There are all kinds of words that are difficult to spell, but thinking about the root word can help. For example, medic in medicine will help you to remember to spell the /s/ sound with the letter c.

QUICK TIP

Family roots

A quick way to increase your vocabulary is to find as many words as you can that contain the same root word. Think of these as families of words. For example, a family of "color" words would include: colorful, colorless, colored, colorfast, colorant. Perhaps you can think of even more.

Rooted in the past

Many of our root words come from Latin and ancient Greek. Knowing their meaning in Latin and Greek can help us understand the longer words in which they appear. For example, the word chrono comes from a Greek work meaning "time." So, it makes sense that it appears in these words:

chronology (a list of events in time order)
synchronize (to make things happen at the same time)

The word colossal (meaning "vast in size") comes from the Greek work colossus, which described a giant statue. The Romans used the Greek word to name their huge amphitheater, the Colosseum, in Rome.

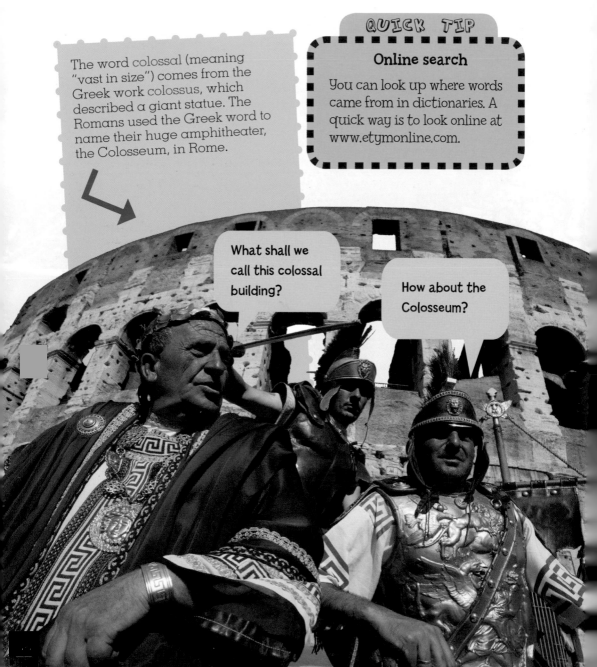

Fill in the gaps

Can you complete these words by choosing one of the words below? The meanings of these words will help you. Check the words you have made in a dictionary afterward.

biblio (Greek) = book
terr (Latin) = earth
auto (Greek) = self

Backstage, he gave me his _____graph.

The _____phile spent every weekend in the bookstore.

The whole _____ain was covered in mud.

Origins

Knowing the original meaning of root words helps us to figure out the meaning of words in which they appear. But beware! Root words can have different meanings. The safest way to find the meaning of a word is by looking it up in a dictionary. The table below shows just a few of the many words that are rooted in Greek and Latin.

Root word	Language it comes from	Meaning	Examples of words that contain the root word
ast	ancient Greek	star	astronomy, astronomer, asterisk
cycle	ancient Greek	circle, wheel, circular motion	bicycle, cyclic, cyclist
port	Latin	carry	transport, portable
vac	Latin	empty	vacuum, vacate
jur or jus	Latin	law	jury, justice, just
tele	ancient Greek	far off, at a distance	telephone, telepathy

Fact!

The /f/ sound in words that came from Greece is spelled as ph. This is because there is no single letter for the /f/ sound in the Greek alphabet.

Prefixes

You can put words in front of root words to change the meaning. The word at the front is called a prefix. Simple prefixes include un-, pre-, and re-. They make things less wordy, so that instead of saying I'm not happy, you can say I'm **un**happy: un (means "not") + happy = unhappy. Here are some more examples:

pre (means "before") + made = premade (made earlier)

re (means "again") + start = restart (start again)

When you add prefixes to the root word, the spelling of the root word does not change.

WORDS IN ACTION

Using words well

If you want to write a story for an action movie or adventure comic, prefixes will be very useful. The two main characters are likely to be the **super**hero (e.g., Batman) and the **anti**hero (e.g., Wolverine). Other words with prefixes you might want to use are: **super**human, **un**earthly, **tele**pathic, **master**mind, **dys**topia, and **mega**city.

Look out for antiaircraft guns!

A superhuman superhero recaptured a dishonest antihero during an antigravity supersonic flight.

There are seven prefixes in this caption. Can you find them?

Prefix problems

Choosing the right prefix is not always easy, because a few prefixes mean similar things. In all the examples below, the prefix means "not":

il- (logical – **il**logical)   im- (possible – **im**possible)
ir- (regular – **ir**regular)   in- (complete – **in**complete)

The prefixes un- and dis- can mean "not," too (e.g., **un**fortunate, **dis**honest). BUT they can also mean to "do the opposite of" (e.g., **un**do, **dis**appear).

Increasing » decreasing «

Prefixes are powerful. They can increase or decrease (make positive or negative) a word's meaning.

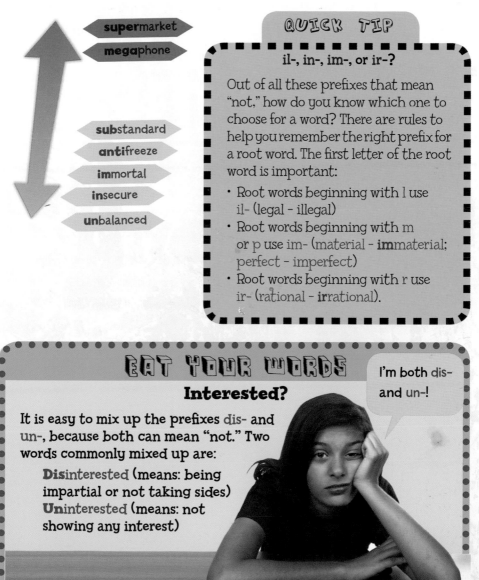

supermarket

megaphone

substandard

antifreeze

immortal

insecure

unbalanced

QUICK TIP

il-, in-, im-, or ir-?

Out of all these prefixes that mean "not," how do you know which one to choose for a word? There are rules to help you remember the right prefix for a root word. The first letter of the root word is important:

- Root words beginning with l use il- (legal - **il**legal)
- Root words beginning with m or p use im- (material - **im**material; perfect - **im**perfect)
- Root words beginning with r use ir- (rational - **ir**rational).

EAT YOUR WORDS

Interested?

I'm both dis- and un-!

It is easy to mix up the prefixes dis- and un-, because both can mean "not." Two words commonly mixed up are:

Disinterested (means: being impartial or not taking sides)
Uninterested (means: not showing any interest)

Ancient beginnings

As with root words, some prefixes in English come from other languages. These prefixes come from Latin:

aqua- (as in **aqua**rium) means "water"
audi- (as in **audi**ence) means "to hear"

These are from ancient Greek words:

tele- (as in **tele**phone) means "far"
micro- (as in **micro**scope) means "small"

Hypno- is from a Greek word meaning "sleep." This prefix is used in words where a sleeplike state is in the meaning, such as hypnosis, hypnotic, and hypnotist. An ancient Greek god called Hypnos was the god of sleep.

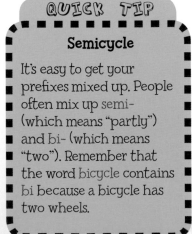

Gives us a clue

The meaning of a prefix can be a helpful clue when you are figuring out the meaning of unfamiliar words. For example, do you know what telephoto means in this sentence?

> Doctor Zap grabbed his camera and focused the telephoto lens on the UFO.

If you don't know what it means, split it up (tele + photo). We know that tele means "far"; we also know that photo is short for "photograph." So, we can guess that a telephoto lens is used to take photographs of things that are far away.

QUICK TIP

Semicycle

It's easy to get your prefixes mixed up. People often mix up semi- (which means "partly") and bi- (which means "two"). Remember that the word bicycle contains bi because a bicycle has two wheels.

Number prefixes

Some prefixes indicate numbers—for example, uni- (one), bi- (two), tri- (three), quadric- (four), and quin- (five). The words below contain number prefixes, too. Can you figure out what each prefix (in bold) means? (If in doubt, look them up in a dictionary.):

centenary   **mill**ennium   **quad**rangle

A **quintet** is a group of five (usually classical) musicians!

QUICK TIP

Guess the meaning

Can you find the right prefix to complete the sentences?

trans- means "through," "across," or "beyond"
sub- means "under"
inter- means "between" or "among"
chron- means "time"

1. The tunnel led them down into a _____ terranean world.
2. The ___ometer recorded the spaceship's journey in milliseconds.
3. The ____parent ghostly wall did not hide the horrors that lay beyond.
4. The girls and the guys soon ____mingled at the party.

Check your answers on page 55.

We use suffixes all the time. A suffix is added to the end of a word to change its meaning. The most common suffix is the letter s, which is added to the end of a word to make it plural— for example, a star and lots of stars.

More than one

Some words need more than the suffix s to make them plural:

- -es is added: box/boxes, motto/mottoes
- -y is replaced with ies: poppy/poppies, spy/spies
- f is replaced with a v: life/lives, knife/knives
- -um becomes a: bacterium/bacteria, curriculum/curricula
- -is becomes es: thesis/theses, emphasis/emphases.

In some cases, the spelling of the root word changes. Examples are foot/feet and person/people. Some words don't need a suffix to become plural—in fact, they don't change at all! Examples are deer and fish.

Mices are smaller than sheeps.

EAT YOUR WORDS

Does it sound right?

It can be hard to get your head around how to use plural suffixes. But soon they come naturally, and often incorrect plurals just don't sound right! There are over 50 common suffixes. You probably actually know most of them already!

Suffixes: Their purposes

Suffixes don't just make words plural. They are useful in many other ways, too—for example, in changing the type of word.

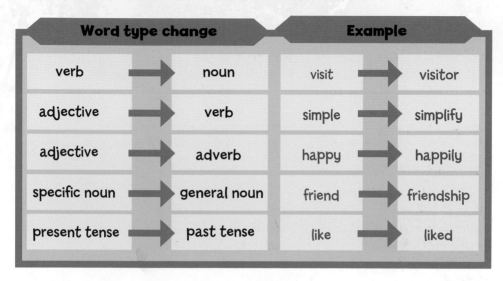

Word type change		Example	
verb ➡	noun	visit ➡	visitor
adjective ➡	verb	simple ➡	simplify
adjective ➡	adverb	happy ➡	happily
specific noun ➡	general noun	friend ➡	friendship
present tense ➡	past tense	like ➡	liked

From noun to adjective or verb

We often change nouns to adjectives by adding suffixes. Many different suffixes change words from a noun to an adjective, such as -ry, -ous, -al, -y, and -ive. For some, there is a change to the spelling of the root word—for example, in fame/fam**ous**, ease/eas**y**, true/tru**ly**, and wonder/wond**rous**.

You can change nouns to verbs by adding -ise/-ize, -ate, -ify, or -en—for example, in light/ligh**ten**, glory/glor**ify**, pollen/pollin**ate**, note/not**ify**, and alphabet/alphabet**ize**.

Spot the suffixes in this poster. The verbs are there to persuade you to do something.

Beautify your home and lighten up your life

Tricky suffixes

Some suffixes are difficult to spell. There are rules that can help you. However, some suffixes are quirky, and so their spelling has to be learned for each individual word, using a dictionary.

Easy to get wrong

The suffixes -ance and -ence mean the same thing: "the quality of/state of." There is no rule to follow to know which is right. Instead, it is a matter of memorizing which spelling matches each word.

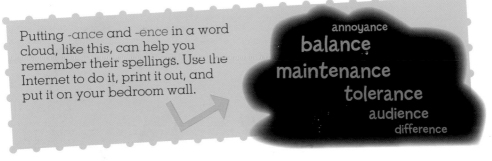

Putting -ance and -ence in a word cloud, like this, can help you remember their spellings. Use the Internet to do it, print it out, and put it on your bedroom wall.

annoyance
balance
maintenance
tolerance
audience
difference

Double letters

Sometimes the last letter of a root word is doubled when adding a suffix. This should be done when a one-syllable word ends in a short vowel and one consonant (e.g., stop, stopping, stopped). But you don't double the last letter when the word ends with more than one consonant (pump, pumped, pumping) or when the root word ends in -e (dance, danced, dancing).

-ible or -able?

The suffixes -ible and -able are very similar. They are also very common, although there are more -able words than -ible words. So, how do you remember which to use? Here are some rules that might help you:

- The -able ending is often used if there is a related word ending in -ation. Examples are commendable (commendation) and justifiable (justification).
- The -able ending is often used if a complete root word exists before it, even if there is no related word ending in -ation. Examples are dependable, comfortable, understandable, reasonable, enjoyable, and noticeable.
- The -ible ending is commonly used if there isn't a complete root word before it. Examples are horrible, incredible, possible, sensible, terrible, and visible. Unfortunately, there are exceptions where the root word is not complete yet has an -able spelling, as in applicable and tolerable. Some people find it helpful to learn spelling rules for suffixes like those above; other people just memorize the spelling of each word!

QUICK TIP

Referal or referral?
Preference or preferrence?

Look at these spellings. Can you spot a reason for doubling the letters in only some of these words?

- preferring, preferred, preference.
- transferring, transferred, transference
- referring, referred, reference

Here are the rules:
The r is doubled if the -fer is still stressed when the ending is added. The r is not doubled if the -fer is no longer stressed. Say the words above out loud to check.

QUICK TIP

Match the ending

Can you match the root word to the correct suffix:

1. read + -able OR -ible
2. slop + -y OR -ppy
3. entr + -ence OR -ance

Check your answers on page 55.

Are we danccing?

No, dear, we're dancing.

The word dance has two consonants at the end, so you don't double the last letter of the root word in dancing.

Table of useful suffixes

Suffix	Purpose	Examples
-s and -es	Added to nouns to make them plural; added to verbs	dogs, bushes, helps, catches
-d, -ed	Added to verbs to change the tense to the past	hopped, hoped, danced
-ful	Added to nouns to change them into adjectives	careful, painful, playful, restful beautiful
-er	Added to verbs to denote the person doing the action and to adjectives to give the comparative form	runner, reader, writer, stronger, faster
-est	Added to adjectives for comparison	biggest, slowest, happiest, latest
-ly	Added to adjectives to form adverbs	sadly, happily, brightly, lately
-ment	Added to verbs to form nouns	payment, advertisement, development
-ness	Added to adjectives to form nouns	darkness, happiness, sadness
-y	Added to nouns to form adjectives	funny, smoky, sandy
-ion, -tion, -ian, -ation, -ition	Added to make a word into an act or process	attraction, occasion
-ing	Added to make a verb into the present tense	running, singing
-ible, -able	Added to nouns to form adjectives	comfortable, terrible

Strange inventions

Language is always changing, and so is the use of suffixes. Many new verbs have been made by adding -ise or -ize to a noun.

Some new words that have appeared recently on the Internet or in speech are listed below. Although we know -ise/ize means to change something or go through a process, the meaning of the following words is unclear. The words have not yet become formally accepted, so they are not in dictionaries. We can only guess at their meaning:

- vampirize—make something look like a vampire?
- Facebookize—put something on the social networking site?
- calenderize—make into a calendar format?
- technologize—make it into a form that can be used by technology?

It is better not to use words like these formally, such as in essays, until they appear in a well-known dictionary.

Using words well

Just for fun, try making up your own words using prefixes and suffixes. Remember that they have to make some sort of sense, so check the meanings of the prefixes and suffixes you plan to use. The root word should be spelled the same as when it is used on its own. Here are some examples:

superantiheroicism
autolazyness
megadelightfulication

Prefixes + suffixes

Some words contain both suffixes and prefixes. Many begin with the prefixes un-, re- and dis-:

un + success + ful
dis + appoint + ment
re + construct + ion

The person who wrote this sign added -ize to alter, when the word alter is perfectly correct on its own!

ALTERIZE *and* **CUSTOMIZE** *your clothes here*

ask our specialists inside for details

What's Missing?

In Standard English, an apostrophe is sometimes used in place of letters to shorten a word or words. These are called contractions, and some are very common. They are often used to show how casually we say some words. For example, instead of saying the two words It is, we often run them together as It's.

Missing parts

Common contractions (in which apostrophes are used for missing letters) are listed here. They are often used in casual writing or in speech—for example, when a character speaks in a story.

can't	is short for	cannot
it's	is short for	it is/it has
didn't	is short for	did not
couldn't	is short for	could not
who's	is short for	who is/who has
she'd	is short for	she did/she would
he'll	is short for	he will
I'm	is short for	I am
isn't	is short for	is not
you're	is short for	you are

QUICK TIP

It's "it is," isn't it?

People often get confused when using it's and its. Remember:
- it's means "it is"
- its means "belonging to it."

Jazz fest!!

'N' BLUES

The word 'n' is short for and. It is used in phrases such as rhythm 'n' blues and rock 'n' roll.

ROCK 'N' ROLL

Using words well

Some people speak using shortened versions of lots of words to sound cool.

Shortening words to one syllable might make them sound more memorable and cool, but it should not be done in formal writing or essays.

I was 'n the park wi' my sk'bord. D'y'know wha' 'm saying', man?!

No, man, I have no idea.

Abbreviations

Standard abbreviations without apostrophes are also common. Instead, periods are used. Many are shortened versions of a Latin phrase:

- a.m. = ante meridiem (before noon)
- p.m. = post meridiem (after noon)
- etc. = et cetera (and the rest/and so on)
- e.g. = exempli gratia (for example)
- i.e. = id est (that is)

Speak easy

Do you play with the structure of words when texting your friends? People often shorten words when writing messages on their cell phones or computers. It is called text speak, textese, or SMS (short message service) language. The words are shortened by taking out the vowels—for example, cmptr (computer) and frnd (friend). Letters are sometimes used for a word where the name of the letter sounds like the word (for example, c = see and u = you).

Instead of words, capital letters are also used. Popular abbreviations in text speak are:

```
LOL = laugh[ing] out loud or lots of love
IMHO = in my humble/honest opinion
VBS = very big smile
BFF = best friends forever
TTYL = talk to you later
```

Sometimes numbers with the same sound (phoneme) as a word are used, such as 4 for the word for, and 2 for to or too:

```
B4N = bye for now
14AA41 = one for all and all for one
2G2BT = too good to be true
2nite = tonight
2moro = tomorrow
```

Abbreviations like these can have more than one meaning, so the context is used to understand what is said. For example, LOL means both lots of love and laughing out loud. In this sentence, the most likely meaning is lots of love: HPPY BDAY! LOL S x

Acronyms

The names of organizations and groups are often shortened into a string of capital letters. Each letter is the first letter of a complete word and helps form made-up words called acronyms. It is much easier and quicker to say UNESCO than the full name of the organization (United Nations Educational, Scientific, and Cultural Organization)!

Some words that now appear without capitals were originally acronyms:

laser = **L**ight **A**mplification by **S**timulated **E**mission of **R**adiation
radar = **RA**dio **D**etection **A**nd **R**anging
scuba = **S**elf-**C**ontained **U**nderwater **B**reathing **A**pparatus

WORDS in ACTION

POEM

Acronyms can be confusing because some are used to mean lots of different things. The acronym POEM, for example, can mean one of ten things! Here are just a few:

Physical **O**ceanography of the **E**astern **M**editerranean
Polar-**O**rbit **E**arth Observation **M**ission
Peripheral **O**riginal **E**quipment **M**anufacturer

If we all spoke in acronyms, life would be very confusing!

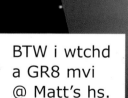

Not everyone would understand this message, and let's hope the writer remembers how to spell watched and movie!

BTW i wtchd a GR8 mvi @ Matt's hs. Will TTYL abt it. Was LOL. B4N

Hyphens (-) break up or link words. Sometimes hyphens are a matter of personal choice or style. Different countries, dictionaries, and companies, such as publishers, decide on whether to put a hyphen between some root words and their prefixes.

Prefixes and hyphens

People tend not to include a hyphen after prefixes such as co-, pre-, mid-, non-, and anti-. But sometimes a hyphen is inserted if the prefix ends in a vowel and the root word starts with a vowel, such as in re-enter and anti-intellectual. It is also used in proper nouns, such as un-American.

In some cases, there are arguments for and against a hyphen, and both with and without is correct in different places.

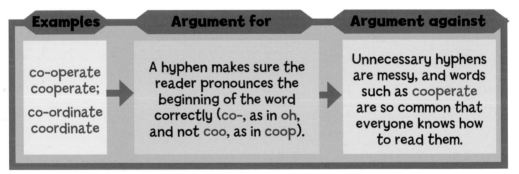

Examples	Argument for	Argument against
co-operate cooperate; co-ordinate coordinate	A hyphen makes sure the reader pronounces the beginning of the word correctly (co-, as in oh, and not coo, as in coop).	Unnecessary hyphens are messy, and words such as cooperate are so common that everyone knows how to read them.

Line breaks

Printed words don't always fit on a line of text in a book, so a last word may be split up and a hyphen added. So that the reader does not lose the flow of the word, the split is usually put between syllables.

A bad word break:

> She heard the ble-
> ating of the lambs
> and took them back
> to the farm.

A better word break:

> She heard the bleat-
> ing of the lambs and
> took them back to
> the farm.

The bad word break makes you start to read the word bleat incorrectly.

To hyphenate or not to hyphenate?

The word or phrase	To hyphenate or not	The reason why
prehistoric pre-historic	✗	The word is so widely used it would be wrong to add a hyphen.
resign re-sign	?	It depends if you mean resign (leave your job) or sign something again (re-sign).
ultra-violet ultraviolet	?	Both are correct and mean the same thing. In the United States, there is usually no hyphen.
hyperlink hyper-link	✗	The word is so widely used it would be wrong to add a hyphen.
non-Catholic	✔	Use a hyphen where the root word has a capital letter.

QUICK TIP

Recover or re-cover?

The choice whether to add a hyphen or not can be essential to the meaning of the word. Read the following sentence and decide whether a hyphen makes better sense:

I have to re-cover/recover the jam to keep the flies away.

A hyphen is essential here, or it becomes a word with a completely different meaning (re-cover = put a cover on again; recover = get well again).

Lunch-time play-group team-leaders required for pre-term high-school activities.

Too many hyphens can look messy and just aren't necessary.

Look It Up!

Whether you want to look up the meaning, spelling, or history of a word, you will find your answer in one of these reference books or lists: a dictionary, a thesaurus, or a glossary. All these resources focus on words, but how do they differ? What sort of information do they contain?

Dictionaries

A dictionary is a book containing a list of the words in a language. The words are in alphabetical order, and for each word there is a definition (an explanation of what the word means). Dictionaries may also include some or all of the following for each word:

- other words that mean the same (synonyms)
- quotations from published texts, to show how the word can be used
- a pronunciation guide (the phonemes in the word)
- a breakdown of the word's structure, such as its syllables
- the history of the word
- how it has changed in meaning through time.

Special dictionaries, such as geography dictionaries, focus on words related to a particular subject.

Thesauruses

A thesaurus is a book that lists words with similar meanings (synonyms) in groups. They are useful when you cannot remember a word or when you want to make a sentence more interesting. For example, with the help of a thesaurus you could rewrite The Sun was hot and the food was tasty as The Sun was sizzling and the food was mouthwatering.

Some thesauruses list words with opposite meanings, too. Words with opposite meanings are called antonyms.

Look up a word in a thesaurus and surprise your friends with some unusual (or exceptional or unparalleled) alternatives!

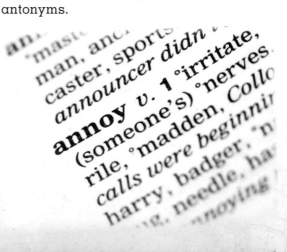

Glossaries

A glossary is an alphabetical list of difficult words, or words linked to specific subjects and their meanings. See page 52 for the glossary in this book.

Online words

There are lots of dictionaries, thesauruses, and glossaries on the Internet. Ask your teacher for recommendations about which are the best to use. Also see page 54 for suggestions.

See page 52

see page 54

QUICK TIP

Cyber search

A quick way to find the meaning of a word on the Internet is to go to Google.com. Type in your word (or a guess and its spelling) followed by definition. Then click "Google search." However, remember that there is a lot of incorrect information on the Internet, so check that the definition you find makes sense in the context.

WORDS IN ACTION

Dictionaries for dummies

Here's how you look up the meaning of a word in a dictionary:

1. Look up the first letter and find that in the dictionary.
2. Run down the words in the dictionary beginning with that letter until you find the second letter in the word you are looking up.
3. Then run down those words until you come to the third letter in your word. Continue in this way until you find your word.
4. If you don't know how to spell your word, take a guess. Then look for it in the same way as above. Your guess might be correct!
5. If you have no idea how to spell a word, look up a word with a similar meaning that you can spell. For example, if you want to find the spelling of pseudonym but don't know where in the dictionary to start, look up the word name. The word pseudonym may be listed as a synonym.

How to read a dictionary

Some dictionaries contain a lot of information about the structure and meaning of words. Here are explanations of some of the information you might find when you look up a word.

This tells you there are two entries for the word stampede; the first is for the noun stampede.

The word at the top is the word you have looked up.

This mark shows the division of the syllables, so you can see that stampede has two syllables (stam/pede).

Symbols are sometimes used to show the sounds in word. You will find an explanation of the syllables in the dictionary. Here, ē means ea, as in easy.

This tells you how to sound out the word.

This is the type of word, e.g., noun, adjective.

The etymology of the word is its history and origin. Often different parts of a word have different origins.

Words often have more than one meaning, depending on the context e.g., whether it relates to animals or people.

This is the second entry for the word stampede; this is for the verb form of the word.

This shows different forms of the word.

Here are two definitions for the verb stampede.

¹stampede
Pronunciation: stam-'pēd
Function: *noun*
Etymology: from a word in the Spanish of Mexico and the American Southwest, *estampida* "stampede," from Spanish *estampida* "a crash, loud noise," from *estamper* "to pound, stamp"
1 : a wild rush or flight of frightened animals
2 : a sudden movement of a crowd of people

²stampede
Function: *verb*
Inflected Form(s): **stam·ped·ed; stam·ped·ing**
1 : to run away or cause (as cattle) to run away in panic
2 : to act together or cause to act together suddenly and without thought

Dictionaries vary in how they set out information. When you use a new dictionary, read any instructions or the introduction to make sure you know how to use it.

Word blind? Arachnophobia

Can you answer these questions using this dictionary entry below and what you have already learned?

1. How many syllables are in arachnophobia?
2. Which language does the word come from?
3. What is the prefix? What is the root word?

See page 55 for the answers.

a·rach·no·pho·bi·a
ə-răk'nə-fōbē-ə-
noun
an abnormal fear of spiders
Etymology: arachn(id) from Greek *arakhnē*
(which means "spider") + phobia from Greek
phobos (which means "fear")
Other forms: adj. a·rach·no·pho·bic or noun
a·rach·no·pho·be

If you're arachnophobic you won't be reading this! See how many other "phobia" words you can find—people fear all kinds of things!

Context

If you are reading and come across a word you don't understand, you can look it up in a dictionary. Or can you? What if you are lying on a beach or stuck on a desert island with no dictionary?

Looking at the meaning of the rest of the text in which the difficult word is set can help. It might be possible to make a good guess. Also, looking at different parts of the word (familiar prefixes or suffixes) can be helpful, too.

Malapropisms

People often make a mistake and get a section of a word wrong when they are talking. These are called malapropisms. But the listener can usually figure out what they are trying to say.

WORDS IN ACTION

Mixed up but meaningful

Research shows that good readers guess most of what they read. Researchers mixed up letters so that only the first and last letter of each word was in the right order. Can you understand any of this?

Aoccdrnig to a rscheearch at an Elingsh uinervtisy, it deosn't mttaer in waht oredr the ltteers in a wrod are, the olny iprmoatnt tihng is taht teh frist and lsat ltteer are in the rghit pclae.

It is better not to use this way of spelling, obviously!

I love the crunchy neutrons in this salad.

The ghost is a pigment of your imagination.

Etymological dictionary

Etymological dictionaries tell you in detail about the history of words—their origins and how they developed into the words we use. Here is an example of an entry:

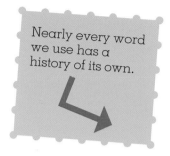

Nearly every word we use has a history of its own.

awesome
awe comes from an Old English word ege (meaning "dread"). It became agi in Middle English; awesome first appeared in the 16th century. It meant "filled with awe." Today awesome is often used to mean "incredible" or "amazing."

Rhyming dictionary

If you are a poet, you will find a rhyming dictionary very useful. It focuses on the end syllables of words and groups together those that rhyme. As with all types of dictionary, you can find rhyming dictionaries on the Internet.

QUICK TIP

What does your name mean?

Some names contain a root word that comes from another language. You can find it by typing your name into a name dictionary on the Internet. Here's an example (not all names have old origins).

Oliver:
Meaning & History
From *Olivier*, a Norman French form of a Germanic name such as ALFHER or an Old Norse name such as *Áleifr* (see OLAF). The spelling was altered by association with Latin *oliva* "olive tree." In the Middle Ages the name became well known in Western Europe because of the French epic *La Chanson de Roland*, in which Olivier was a friend and advisor of the hero Roland.
DIMINUTIVES: Oli, Ollie (English)
FEMININE FORMS: Alivia, Olivia, Olyvia (English).

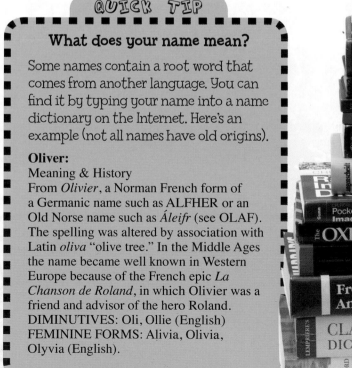

A Very Brief History of English

The English language first developed in the British Isles, then it spread as people traveled and settled around the world, including North America and Australia. The structure and spelling of English words have changed, and new words have appeared over hundreds of years. Many words we use today are rooted in the distant past. Ancient warriors and invaders spoke earlier versions of some words we speak today.

500–43 BCE: Celtic

The first people to influence English were the Celts—tribes of people in central and northern Europe who spoke a similar language. Few English words are Celtic, although many place names contain Celtic words— for example, glen (which means a narrow valley).

43 BCE–c.450 CE: Latin

The Romans invaded the British Isles, and their language (Latin) has left its mark in spellings and many of the words we use today.

From 449 CE: Old English

Tribes from what are now Germany, Denmark, and the Netherlands began to arrive in the British Isles, including the Angles and the Saxons. Their Anglo-Saxon language is now called Old English. We still use a third of Anglo-Saxon vocabulary today. These include words such as food, house, and night.

From 789 CE: Norse

The invading Viking warriors from Scandinavia settled and brought almost 2,000 new words with them. Their Norse language is found in the origin of words such as egg and smile. They also introduced the letter k.

From 1066: French

After the Norman Conquest, French was spoken by the rulers and elite for hundreds of years. Thousands of our words originate from French. These include:

- many words in which the /sh/ sound is spelled ch (chef, chute, chalet, machine).

- words ending with the /g/ sound spelled -gue and the /k/ sound spelled -que (e.g. league, colleague; antique, unique).

From the 1500s: Latin and Greek

New interest in the languages of ancient Rome and ancient Greece brought many more Latin and also Greek words into our language. Greek words include those with the /k/ sound spelled ch (e.g., school, chorus, chemist, character).

In about 1450, the first books were printed. Printers made their own spelling rules, and so spellings started to become fixed.

English poet and playwright, William Shakespeare (1564-1616) is credited with bringing many words into the English language, such as advertising, lackluster, and swagger. Some of the new words were made by putting words together for the first time—for example, lack+luster. However, we can't be sure that Shakespeare invented them. He may just be credited with the words because his texts have had so much attention.

From the 1800s: American English

From the 1800s, American English was starting to become noticeably different from British English (for example, the U.S. spelling of theater and British spelling theatre). More words from around the world became part of Standard English vocabulary, too.

Early letterpress printing machines like this were very slow to use. Every letter (each was a letter-shaped block) had to be put in position before ink was applied and paper pressed over the top.

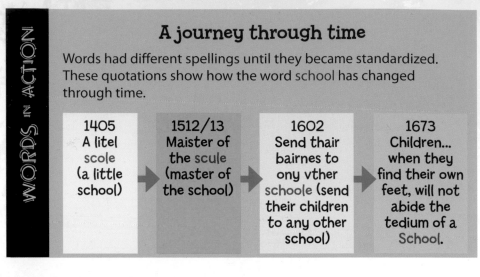

A journey through time

Words had different spellings until they became standardized. These quotations show how the word school has changed through time.

1405	1512/13	1602	1673
A litel scole (a little school)	Maister of the scule (master of the school)	Send thair bairnes to ony vther schoole (send their children to any other school)	Children... when they find their own feet, will not abide the tedium of a School.

New inventions

New words have been created to name new inventions, using ancient prefixes or suffixes. For example, the first cars were called automobiles, made from the Greek word auto (meaning "self") and the Latin word mobils (meaning "moving"). The word locomotive was first used when a moving railroad steam engine was invented. The word is made from the Latin word loco (meaning "from a place") and the Latin motivus (meaning "causing motion").

automobile
1. A public passenger vehicle having its own means of propulsion, esp. a tramcar that combines engine and carriage. Cf. motor car n. 1. Now disused.

Words from around the world

The more people traveled, the more words from different languages were shared. Here are a few words from around the world that have become Standard English words, too.

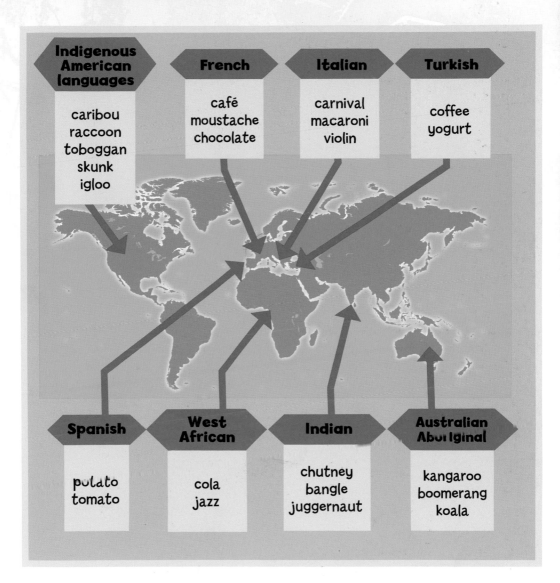

Indigenous American languages
caribou
raccoon
toboggan
skunk
igloo

French
café
moustache
chocolate

Italian
carnival
macaroni
violin

Turkish
coffee
yogurt

Spanish
potato
tomato

West African
cola
jazz

Indian
chutney
bangle
juggernaut

Australian Aboriginal
kangaroo
boomerang
koala

A living language

English has traveled the world for hundreds of years, and it continues to change because it is a living language—a language that changes to fulfill our changing needs. While the rules of Standard English are necessary for a shared understanding and clear communication, they do not limit words or make them less exciting. Words are the most valuable tools we have.

Phonemes and Graphemes

You can refer to this list of more complicated phonemes and graphemes to help you to figure out spellings and sound out words correctly. The example words should help, too.

Phoneme	Grapheme	Example words
/d/	d, dd, -ed	dig, daddy, pulled
/f/	f, ff, ph, gh	fit, bluff, photo, rough
/h/	h, wh	hat, who
/j/	j, g, dg	jot, giant, badge
/k/	k, c, ck, ch, qu	kitten, cat, duck, school, mosquito
/m/	m, mm, mb, mn	map, mummy, lamb, autumn
/n/	n, nn, gn, kn	not, runny, gnat, knock
/r/	r, rr, wr, rh	rat, berry, write, rhyme
/s/	s, ss, c, sc, st	son, moss, cell, scent, listen
/t/	t, tt, -ed, th, bt	tap, button, jumped, Thomas, doubt
/w/	w, u, o	wag, penguin, one
/y/	y, i	yes, onion
/z/	z, zz s, se, ze, ss, x	zap, buzz, is, please, seize, scissors, xylophone
/e/	e, ea, sai, ay, ie, eo, a	hen, head, said, says, befriend, leopard, many
/i/	i, y, o, u, ui	it, gym, women, busy, build
/o/	o, a	on, was

/u/	u, o u-e, ou, oe, oo	run, son, come, young, does, flood
/ch/	ch, tch	chop, catch
/ng/	ng, n (before k), ngue	bring, plank, tongue
/sh/	sh, s, ss, t (before -ion and -ial), ci, ch, ce	ship, sure, mission, attention, partial, special, chef, ocean
/th/$_1$	th	think
/th/$_2$	th, the	then, breathe
/zh/	s (before -ure and -ion), su, ige	revision, treasure, usual, beige
/ai/	ai, ay, a-e	rain, day, fake
/ar/	ar, a, al, are, hear	farm, father, palm, are, hearth
/air/	air, are, ear, ere	pair, dare, bear, there
/ear/	ear, eer, ere, ier	fear, deer, here, pier
/ee/	ee, ea, e, ie, e-s-e, eo	three, pea, he, chief, these, people
/igh/	igh, ie, y, i-e, i, eigh, ye, y-e	right, tie, my, ripe, find, height, I, bye, type
/oa/	oa, ow, o, oe, o-e, oh, ough, ol	float, grow, toe, go, bone, oh, though, folk
/oo/$_1$	oo, ew, ue, u-e, o, ough, wo, o-e	root, few, blue, rule, to, through, two, lose
/oo/$_2$	oo, u, ou	look, put, could
/or/	or, aw, au, augh, oor, ore, al, ough, ou, oa	for, raw, Paul, caught, poor, more, talk, brought, four, abroad
/oi/	oi, oy	coin, boy
/ur/	various	motor, pillar, thorough

Glossary

abbreviation word that is shortened or written in a way that shows how it is pronounced

acronym word or name that is made from the first letters of words, such as NATO (North Atlantic Treaty Organization)

adjective word used to describe, or modify, a noun or pronoun

adverb word that describes, or modifies, a verb or another adverb

American English English language in the United States, which has its own accent and dialects, plus specific spellings and grammar

antonym word that has an opposite meaning from others

apostrophe punctuation mark that shows who owns something (the girl's book) or that part of a word is missing (can't)

British English English language in the British Isles, which has its own accent and dialects, plus specific spellings and grammar

compound word word made up of two or more smaller words

consonant any letter in the alphabet that is not a vowel; y is sometimes used as a consonant and sometimes as a vowel

context subject or sentence in which a word is used

definition meaning of a word

dialect form of a language in which pronunciation, grammar, and vocabulary are different from the standard

dictionary book or online web site with words listed in alphabetical order, giving various information about each

emphasis loudness or weight of voice

encyclopedia book (or set of books) or web site that has many different types of information, organized by subject and in alphabetical order

etymology origin of words; also the study of words

glossary alphabetical list of words and their meanings

grapheme letter or letters that represent the sounds that make up words

haiku simple Japanese poem, usually with three lines

homophones words that have the same sounds and spelling but different meanings

hyphen short dash that is used to link parts of words or to link the words in a phrase

indigenous native to a country or area

Latin language originally used by the ancient Romans

malapropism mistaken use of a word, often because the speaker is confused about two words that sound similar

morphology structure of words

noun word that names a person, place, thing, feeling, quality, or idea

phoneme unit of sound when you speak; spoken words are made up of one or more phonemes

plural more than one

prefix syllable or word at the front of a root word

pronounce say a word in a specific way

pronunciation way in which words are sounded out

rap music rhyming verse spoken to the rhythm of music

rhyme words that rhyme have endings that sound the same (although the endings are not always spelled the same)

rhythm sound of words when some or parts of the words are spoken as stressed and unstressed

root word basic part of a word, from which others can be built—for example, by adding a prefix, a suffix, or both

short vowel one of the five single letter vowels in the alphabet (a, e, i, o, u) that have a short sound in words (as in hot) rather than a long vowel sound (as in coat)

silent letter individual letter (or letters) in words that does not sound out and cannot be heard when the word is spoken, such as gh in light

SMS (text speak) vocabulary and grammar used for texts and other online messaging

Standard English accepted English language (with spelling, pronunciation, and grammar rules) of an English-speaking country

stressed when emphasis is put on a word or part of a word when it is spoken

suffix syllable or word at the end of a root word

syllable word or part of a word that has a separate sound when you say it

synonym word that has the same or similar meaning to another word or words

tense form of verb that shows the timing of events—for example, past tense or future tense

thesaurus type of dictionary in which words with the same and similar meanings are grouped together

verb word that expresses the action or state of a noun or pronoun

vocabulary all the words of a language or dialect

vowel letters a, e, i, o, and u; y is also sometimes used as a vowel

Find Out More

Books

Baker, Rosalie. *In a Word: 750 Words and Their Fascinating Stories and Origins*. Peterborough, N.H.: Cobblestone/Carus, 2006.

Cook, Vivian. *Accomodating Brocolli in the Cemetary or Why Can't Anybody Spell?* New York: Simon & Schuster, 2005.

Muschla, Gary Robert. *Exploring Grammar* (Practice Makes Perfect). New York: McGraw Hill, 2011.

Webster's Student Dictionary and Thesaurus. New York: Reader's Digest, 2007.

Web sites

www.behindthename.com
Have fun finding out about the origin of your name or your friends' names.

www.etymonline.com
Learn more about the origin of words.

www.wordcentral.com
This is Merriam-Webster's site for kids, and it offers a dictionary and thesaurus.

Further topics to research

- What does Middle English look like? Read some of the writings of the author Geoffrey Chaucer. How much of his work do you understand?

- Look at documents from early in the history of the United States, such as the Declaration of Independence. How much has American English changed in the last 200-plus years? How has it stayed the same?

- Read about the history of important dictionaries such as Merriam-Webster. How have they helped shape the development of the English language?

Answers

Page 20: Compound words

The root words are underlined:

playground
farmyard
bedroom
blackberry
dragonfly

Page 27: Guess the meaning

1. subterranean
2. chronometer
3. transparent
4. intermingled

Page 31: Match the ending

1. readable
2. sloppy
3. entrance

Page 43: Word blind? Arachnophobia

1. Six syllables: a/rach/no/pho/bi/a
2. Greek
3. Prefix: arachno; root word: phobia

Index